FROM PIECES to PEACE

Kyle Edwards

Copyright © 2007 by Kyle Edwards

From Pieces to Peace
by Kyle Edwards

Printed in the United States of America

ISBN 978-1-60477-219-7

All rights reserved solely by the author. The author guarantees all contents are original and do not infringe upon the legal rights of any other person or work. No part of this book may be reproduced in any form without the permission of the author. The views expressed in this book are not necessarily those of the publisher.

Unless otherwise indicated, Bible quotations are taken from the Holy Bible, New International Version®. NIV®. Copyright © 1973, 1978, 1984 by International Bible Society. Used by permission of Zondervan.

www.xulonpress.com

Dedication

I dedicate this book to all the wounded and broken individuals who have experienced or been affected by an abortion, to anyone who has lost a baby and not been able to move on, and to anyone who thinks sin in their life is too great for God to forgive.

Thank you to my family and friends for their encouragement to finish this book. Bonnie, the pictures are perfect. Thank you for hearing my heart.

A special thank you to my son. You will never know how much I love you, and I am so privileged to be your mom. You are truly a gift from God.

Thank you to Doug (my ex-husband) for being such a good friend over the last few years. The Lord does heal old wounds.

And to my greatest love and encourager, thank You, Lord, for the courage and the words You have spoken to bring freedom and forgiveness to my life and now to others.

Contents

    Introduction ix
1 My Story 13
2 Post-Abortion Syndrome 21
3 The 5 R's 29
4 Broken Silence 37
5 Pieces to Peace 41
6 Freedom 45
7 It Is Finished 49
Conclusion 53
Celebration 61

Introduction

1973, *Roe v. Wade*. The legalizing of abortion. A decision to allow a woman to have free choice in determining the life of her baby. A law, a rule of conduct or action that changed the lives of millions of victims.

A right: in accordance with or conformable to the law; the arguable "right to choose" that deceptively led women into a decision without full knowledge of the risks involved. Not only physically but emotionally and psychologically as well.

A choice: to select, the opportunity, right, or power to choose. We live in the "land of the free" where we can freely exercise our choices and not have to suffer the consequences of the law, as long as the law is followed.

Abortion: a resolution for "quick relief" of an issue without regard to the crippling consequences that accompany this decision.

A decision that has left millions of women emotionally paralyzed, sometimes for their entire life, because of lack of knowledge and understanding.

Abortion is the termination of pregnancy. To terminate: end, finish, abolish, cease, stop, expire, culminate. To take the life of a baby.

In our society, abortion is an acceptable option to giving birth. By the age of forty-five, 43 percent of women in the United States have had one abortion. Repeat abortions were 20 percent in 1973 but rose to 44 percent in 1987. By 2000, 47 percent of all abortions in the United States were repeats.[1]

There are several types of abortions. The way an abortion is performed depends on the length of the pregnancy. Ninety percent of abortions occur in the first twelve weeks of pregnancy. In 2000, 1.31 million pregnancies were terminated by abortion in the United States, with women in their twenties accounting for 56 percent of these abortions.[2]

The type or length of pregnancy does not matter. It results in the same thing—death. Death not only of the infant but also part of the mother. I have heard time and time again from women who have had abortions that when they terminated their pregnancy a part of them died as well, leaving an inexplicable void, a void for something that has never been filled.

My heart stirs with urgency for women to find freedom and forgiveness. There is destruction of a life when an abortion takes place, not only the baby's but also the woman's. The baby is part of the woman; therefore how can she not be affected? Have you been paying the psychological price for the pain, shame, and alienation of an abortion?

This is not a book to discuss women's rights, or anti- or pro-abortion issues, but one to reveal the after-effects of an abortion. This book also unveils the freedom available from the psychological and emotional chains of oppression. Women choose to have an abortion for many reasons. I am not here to condemn or pass judgment on anyone who has had an abortion. I have been there—or should I say, I am still there.

I have found freedom from the emotional terror that haunted me for years, and I want others to know they can find this freedom also. Sharing my story may only affect the life of one person. If it is only one, then it is worth it!

We are hard pressed on every side, but not crushed; perplexed, but not in despair; persecuted, but not abandoned; struck down, but not destroyed.
2 Corinthians 4:8-9

Endnotes:

1. S. Henshaw et al., Ab. Characteristics, 1994-95, *Fam. Plan. Persp.*, Vol. 28, No. 4, July '96, p.143
2. Jones RK, Darroch JE and Henshaw SK, Patterns in the socioeconomic characteristics of women obtaining abortions in 2000-2001, *Perspectives on Sexual and Reproductive Health*, 2002, 34(5):226-235.

Chapter 1

My Story

I was the youngest of three girls, the tomboy in the family. We lived in the same town and home throughout our childhood and school years. Growing up was fun as we went on family vacations, and camping trips, and my parents loved to entertain friends.

As a small child I was, as some would say, strong-willed. As a teenager, I moved to the next level, known as rebellious. If I did not want to do something, I was not going to be forced into it. If I wanted to do something, you bet I did it!

As a young girl I knew that I wanted to be a nurse when I grew up, so that's what I did. After graduating from high school at the age of seventeen, I went to nursing school. I met my husband during our senior year of high school and our relationship continued. After I completed nursing school, we were married. I was nineteen, he was twenty.

I was so excited to be married and to be moving on in life. So many desires, so many hopes, so many dreams, but in a very short time that all changed.

It has been twenty-eight years since I discovered I was pregnant with my first child. I was happy but shocked, especially being a newlywed of six weeks. I waited until my husband came home from work, and after dinner I gave him the happy news. Anticipating his surprise, an excited, nervous feeling overcame me.

His reaction was anything but what I had anticipated. He was irate! There was no discussion, there was no acknowledging that I had a baby, our baby, inside of me. He insisted on an abortion. I told him I did not want an abortion and the argument escalated until I was thrown up against the wall, held by the throat, and told I had no choice in the matter.

I could not wrap my mind around what was happening. I could not believe my ears or begin to understand how such a happy time in life could be so completely interrupted by this anger. Who was this man that I had promised just six weeks earlier to live with for the rest of my life?

My world was caving in all around me, as if I were a child again and being punished for doing something wrong. I did not want the abortion. I was so intimidated and desperately needed someone to talk to. Who could possibly understand what I did not even understand? I had never seen this side of my husband before. *Surely this behavior will pass and he will change his mind*, I thought.

From Pieces to Peace

As the days and weeks passed, the physical and verbal abuse continued and became worse. Where did this abuse stem from? The marriage? The pregnancy? There was no sign of violence before we married. What happened?

I was so alone. I had no close friends. We had recently moved into a neighborhood about twenty miles from my hometown. I felt that I had no place to go and no one to confide in. The sense of alienation and seclusion was horrifying. Walking on eggshells every day, not knowing what kind of reaction would come from him in any given situation, was exhausting.

Each day my husband would ask me if the appointment for the abortion was scheduled. He told me he was taking me to make sure the abortion was done. I made the appointment thinking I could still change his mind before we arrived, but every time I tried to speak about the baby I was shut down like a car coming to a screeching halt. The coercion and threats continued and increased in intensity. I went to the abortion clinic on a Saturday in December.

The ride was completely silent. I remember thinking, *There is no way out of this.* Maybe the nurse would say something that would cause him to change his mind. The hopelessness was overpowering. I filled out the necessary paperwork and sat in the waiting area until a nurse came to get me. There was no explanation of the procedure, nor was I given a choice.

I was escorted down a corridor into a cold room, as if I were heading for my own execution. "Take off your clothes and put on this gown," the nurse grumbled. "Sit on the exam table, and the doctor will be in shortly." I was anticipating some type of explanation about the procedure. Certainly, these people knew what informed consent was. I had a right to know—or did I? Some people choose not to know, others choose to ignore, but they still have a choice.

An informed consent is both a legal and an ethical principle. The consent is a process through which accurate and relevant information is presented to an individual so that she is able to knowledgeably accept or forego medical care, based on an appreciation and understanding of the facts presented.[1]

The wait seemed like an eternity. I remember thinking, *This room is so plain.* The atmosphere was dreary and lifeless and the room had only a few pieces of equipment in it. There was a glass bottle on a machine next to the exam table and a few instruments on the counter space with a large garbage container in the corner. I was cold and shivering, due to the lack of clothing and because of anxiety, fear, and anticipation of the unknown. My mind was moving like the wind in a storm.

Thoughts, like leaves blowing in all directions, some staying a flight and others quickly falling to the ground, flooded my mind. I tried to focus my thoughts on a rational reason for being there, but I was unable to capture the reality of what I was doing.

A few minutes later the doctor entered the exam room and instructed me to lie back and put my legs in the stirrups. My legs were strapped in and the doctor began to examine me. He told me he would insert an instrument inside my uterus that would clean out my uterus. Is this what they refer to as an explanation of the procedure? I did not know what to expect. Then all of a sudden, the machine next to the table was turned on, and without any anesthesia, the doctor inserted this piercing instrument into my uterus, forcing my cervix to open.

The excruciating pain literally took my breath away. I felt as if I were suffocating, and beads of cold sweat rolled off my body from the pain. It felt as if I were being torn apart piece by piece. I cried out "O God!" as I grabbed the sides of the exam table and turned my head to the side, where I saw the glass bottle filling up with blood and shreds of tissue. It was my baby. "Oh, dear God, what have I done?" I cried silently. The pain and the tears intensified with an overwhelming feeling of guilt and shame as the doctor said, "We're almost done."

The procedure ended, and as I sat on the table the nurse removed the equipment and threw the glass bottle into a garbage container filled with other glass bottles. The sound of the glass bottle hitting the others was shattering to my insides. *All those babies*, I thought as the tears rolled down my cheeks. I felt like I was having a nightmare. *When will I wake up from this bad dream?* I never realized I would live this unending nightmare for years to come.

After dressing, I was given instructions and sent home. I was angry! I felt violated, as if I had been raped. I thought, *Now you give instructions!* My husband was waiting for me, and as we left the facility, he walked several feet ahead of me as if he did not know me. Not a word was spoken the entire ride home. I continued to have severe cramping and heavy bleeding. I wanted to hear my husband console me or at least ask "Are you doing okay?"—

I had done what he forced me to do—but that never happened. He left me at home alone that night and went out with his friends. It was as if his life was great, not a worry in the world, and here I was full of shame and guilt. The thought of knowing I did not matter to my husband of less than eight weeks was becoming a reality in my mind and another wound to my heart.

My husband would not allow me to openly grieve after the abortion. If the subject was not discussed, it was easier to deal with. As if it never happened. I feared ongoing or additional abuse if I spoke of the procedure or how I was feeling. It was a subject not to be spoken of.

My tears were always questioned. Was my husband trying to protect me from the pain of remembering, not realizing the pain of loneliness and isolation was worse? I became immobilized and unable to process my feelings. The guilt and shame I felt were devastating. Soon even my tears ceased and I found myself "tearless" because of the bitterness.

I began to believe I deserved everything that came my way because of what I had done. I deserved the abuse by my husband. The emotional and verbal abuse that accompanied the physical abuse was my own punishment.

Not only did I keep my abortion a secret, I also kept the abuse a secret for ten years.

Silence is a powerful thing. The cliché "Silence is golden" became anything but golden to me. The silence said to me that my husband did not care, that I did not matter to him.

Anger and grief obstructed any productive communication, barring any kind of problem solving. The silences of the night became haunting nightmares. My thoughts would race like lightning in a summer storm and yet they could find a place in my mind in which they would never leave. This trap of silence became my voiceless enemy for years.

Endnotes:

1. Misinformed Consent: The Medical Accuracy of State Developed Abortion Counseling Materials; Guttmacher Policy Review, Fall 2006, Volume 9, Number 4

Chapter 2

Post-Abortion Syndrome

My abortion was a pivotal point in my life, but it took me twenty years to realize it. The emotional toll of no conversation surrounding my abortion was too great to conquer. The isolation of the decision to abort our baby and the consequences of that decision have been intense.

Many professionals claim there is no psychological damage as a result of an abortion. I disagree. Reflecting on my own life, I see lifelong reactions that are parallel to the effects of Post-Abortion Syndrome (PAS). I would venture to say I am not alone.

The loss due to an abortion is real and painful. Post-Abortion Syndrome consists of negative and self-destructive behaviors that become a way of life for individuals who experience traumatic stress.

Read the following list of behaviors, and if you have had an abortion and are experiencing any of these, I encourage you to read on.

These behaviors may include:

- guilt
- anger
- shame
- despair
- bitterness
- depression
- helplessness
- hopelessness
- low self-esteem
- sexual dysfunction
- anorexia or bulimia
- drug or alcohol abuse
- frequent bouts of crying
- fear of future pregnancies
- suicidal thoughts or threat
- feelings of distrust or betrayal
- unhealthy or abusive relationships

If you have experienced an abortion and can identify with any of these, you may be suffering from Post-Abortion Syndrome, the inability to process fear, anger, sadness, and grief associated with the loss of an aborted child.

My choice to abort has challenged every ethical, moral, spiritual, and idealistic belief I have. Abandoning these beliefs out of fear or desperation caused chaos in every area of my life. For years, I struggled with the moral and religious values that conflicted with my abortion. Even the fact that abortion was legal did not give me relief from the guilt I lived with. My peace and joy had been snuffed out of my life and was buried like a smoldering fire waiting for oxygen to give it life again.

Statistics show that at least 70 percent of women having abortions say they believe it is immoral. However, they chose against their conscience because of pressure from others and their circumstances.[1]

I thought the never-ending sorrow I experienced was the destiny of my life. Then I read something. It said that my life was predestined. It was predestined before I even existed. This was not new to me as I was raised in a home where the Bible was frequently read, but for the first time I didn't just read it I understood what it was saying.

This passage was telling me there are no accidental births. God meets every baby in the womb of the mother and gives destiny to each one. This is a personal interaction between God and the baby. Listen to this word as you read it.

For you created my inmost being: you knit me together in my mother's womb. I praise you because I am fearfully and wonderfully made: My frame was not hidden from you when I was made in the secret place. When I was woven together in the depths of the earth, your eyes saw my unformed body. All the days ordained for me were written in your book before one came to be.
Psalm 139:13-16

I thought, *Predestined for what?* Predestined to make the capital mistake of a lifetime? To take the life of another human being? Life was not worth living if my destiny was to be shameful and guilt-ridden by painful thoughts and feelings of what I had done.

I kept reading and discovered that when God created man and woman He created them with the ability to choose. Our choices dictate the difficult times in our lives, not our Creator. Can you imagine being created to do and to be only what you were told to do and to be? The creative and sometimes rebellious side of me says "No way!" I like to choose and make my own decisions. Then the logical side of me says, "You have not done so well with your choices and decisions. Maybe if you had listened to someone you would not have gone through so many tough times." However, I did not see that at the time.

Yes, hindsight is 20/20 vision. If we could relive our lives after we have lived it for twenty, thirty, or forty years we would all live it differently in some way. Our lives are created for us to learn as we live, to seek our source of strength and help, to find freedom and then to assist others to get through life. Some of us just learn the hard way. Not because we are incompetent in the way we think but because of the choices we make. We become who we are based on the choices we make. Some good choices and some bad. Our daily decisions determine our destiny.

I did not like who I was becoming. The exterior of a hardhearted, self-dependent, workaholic professional shielding a fearful, shameful, unforgiving, and bitter woman. The bitterness in my heart was causing anger, resentment, and hostility. A person who is bitter cannot keep it a secret. It shows in words, attitudes, and looks. I could not give love or receive love because of the unforgiveness I was harboring that gave breath and life to my malignancy of bitterness.

I was living a double life, putting on whatever mask I needed for that moment just to get through the day. The weariness and imprisonment I lived became unbearable at times, and I wanted to break away from it all. I thought many times about getting into the car and driving and driving and not turning back. I was running from something that seemed to be constantly following me, and because it was locked up inside of me, I could not get away from it.

I wanted to become whom I was truly meant to be—a woman created by God. Nonetheless, I could not do it by myself. I so longed for someone in my life to depend on and to love me for who I was. There is only one person who will always be there, never disappoint me, and always allow me to be who I truly am. Jesus Christ. My Creator. Our Creator.

Never will I leave you or forsake you.
Hebrews 13:5

*Jesus Christ is the same yesterday, today
and forever.*
Hebrews 13:8

Who knows you and can love you better than the One who created you? No one. To imagine that someone has committed His entire life to me, promising to always be there and to never change, is beyond comprehension. The key is that we do not have to understand it, just believe it.

Nineteen years after my abortion a close friend of mine sat with me one afternoon as I openly began to grieve over my aborted baby. Acknowledging the abortion and the pain that hurt so badly at times, with no words to express what I was feeling, broke through the behaviors of denial and avoidance, which are obstacles to healing that prolong psychological and spiritual suffering.

I remember that as she prayed with me I asked the Lord to really forgive me, as I had many times before, but this time we prayed a prayer of dedication of my baby to the Lord. I was so wrapped up in my guilt, pain, and shame that I did not think about the Father in heaven caring for this baby that I had aborted.

I began to see the life I was living and how it was being motivated by guilt. Guilt trips in my relationships for reasons of manipulation, power, or personal gain were flashing through my mind. The unresolved guilt in my own life allowed Satan to keep me bound to the lie that I could not see through the fog to the grace of God.

You see, God motivates by love. God desires a relationship of love, not guilt, manipulation, personal gain or power. This does not excuse me of wrongdoing, but through the prompting of the Spirit of God, as we realize the unparalleled grace and love that come from Him, our response to Him will be one of love and gratitude, not guilt. God is not interested in what we can do for Him. He does not want our sacrifices, or an offering, as it says in the book of Hosea. He wants our love, and He wants us to know Him.

Even in dealing with what we might consider the greatest unforgivable sin, I love to recall what the Bible says: "God's love endures forever." It does not say it just once but multiple times. Read Psalm 136. This phrase is repeated twenty-six times! No matter what we do or have done, God's love is greater. No man or woman on earth compares to God's love. When Jeremiah wrote the book of Lamentations 3:22-23 he wrote,

Because of the Lord's great love we are not consumed, for His [the Lord's] compassions never fail. They [His compassions] are new every morning; great is Your [the Lord's] faithfulness.

God waits for us to ask Him for help. God promises to forgive and to help us. We do not have to live each day with the guilt of sin. When God forgives us, HE FORGIVES US. God does not wait for us to sin again and throw our past sins into our face. He forgives and forgets. Psalm 103:10-12 says,

He does not treat us as our sins deserve or repay us according to our iniquities. For as high as the heavens are above the earth, so great is His love for those who fear Him; as

far as the east is from the west, so far has He removed our transgressions [sins] from us.

This fear referred to is not a human fear. It is not a feeling or emotion of dread or danger. To fear the Lord is to revere Him. Revere means to adore, respect, and worship Him. How do we learn to adore someone? We spend time with Him. The more we learn about God the more we see and experience the love and grace that He so compassionately wants to give us, allowing us to move beyond a life motivated by guilt to a life motivated by true love.

God is the Creator of all, and He created my aborted baby. I remember hearing that the process of healing from abortion is not about who you are and what you have done; it is about who God is and what He has done. This was the beginning of healing in my life. Instead of doubting the mercy and goodness of God, I began to expect it. A new road and new journey began that day. The road less traveled has become a long yet significant journey.

Endnotes:

1. S. Henshaw et al., Ab. Characteristics, 1994-95, *Fam. Plan. Persp.,* Vol. 28, No. 4, July '96

Chapter 3

The 5 R's

There is always a starting point and an end to every situation. I believe the five contributing factors in making a decision to have an abortion are: 1) a reason, 2) the risk, 3) requirements, 4) a response, and 5) the rationalization.

Women's reasons for having an abortion vary from convenience to medical. Some women experience pressure or force from others; this is called coercion. Coercion and forcefulness go a long way when you are in the midst of emotional turmoil.

Never in a thousand years did I ever dream of having an abortion. During my years as a teenager, I was so afraid of the consequences of getting pregnant that I was probably one of very few virgins graduating from high school. When I look back I think, "What happened?" I was quite the rebel growing up, and no one walked all over me. What changed?

We become what we live. A negative environment will eventually blindside you, and you do not even realize it is happening. My self-esteem was so low at the time of my pregnancy that I was not able to stand for what I believed in. I could not even look at myself in the mirror.

Our thoughts are the basic foundation of our character. This influences our choices, which in turn influence our successes and failures.

Many women choose abortion out of fear—fear of losing their partner when the relationship is insecure and raising a baby as a single parent. Some say the loss of control over their lives or the inability to provide for and raise a baby is the reason. Fear of the unknown. Fear can be crippling.

As reported in the Central Illinois Right to Life online newsletter (http://www.cirtl.org) the overwhelmingly majority of abortions (95 percent), are done as a means of birth control. Relief or grief? People look at abortion as a choice that will bring relief, but they do not consider the grief that it brings. The loss in abortion is real and needs to be mourned.

The risk of an abortion includes the physical risks of hemorrhage, infection, perforation of the uterus, and effects on later pregnancies. In some cases the pregnancy is not completely terminated and the pregnancy continues, which can lead to life threatening complications for the mother. In addition to the physical risks are the emotional risks. Initially following an abortion a woman may experience a feeling of relief but then find herself dealing with unexpected emotions. She may, once again, remain silent not knowing how or whom to talk to regarding these feelings.

These emotions are labeled as Post-Abortion Syndrome. The anger, guilt, and shame can lead to reactions of long-term grief, sexual dysfunction, anniversary reactions, broken relationships, memory repression, flashbacks, and—even more severe— hallucinations, increased drug and alcohol use, and suicidal thoughts, as well as the other symptoms already mentioned.

The requirements for having an abortion have changed over the years. Abortions were criminal acts until the legalization of abortion in 1973. At that time a woman had to be an adult to have an abortion. Then underage teens could abort if they had the consent of a parent. Although teen abortion is legal, in the United States, each state varies in its requirements for a legal under-age abortion. States are divided into three categories: 1) states that require parental permission, 2) states that do not require parental permission, and 3) states that require parental notification but do not require their permission. Currently thirty-four states enforce parental consent or notification laws for minors seeking an abortion.[1]

The response of people to one who has experienced an abortion varies depending on their personal ethics and convictions.

The responses addressed here are:

- acceptance
- denial

- lack of understanding
- fear
- busyness

There is either acceptance of an abortion or denial that it was ever done. This widens the gap of understanding, and every woman who has experienced this pain cries out for someone to understand her personal anguish.

The fear of opinionated or religious repercussions and the negative reactions from friends or family keep most women silent about anything they feel after their abortion.

In this day and age of busyness it is so easy to occupy our minds and emotions with daily routines that we do not delve into the silence of our personal and intimate side, which reveals the pain and sorrow that is unnoticed by others. Lack of understanding leads to further avoidance and encourages silence.

Rationalization vs. reason. We are all human, and humans can rationalize anything, especially if it is to our advantage. We can rationalize anything to ease our conscience even before we do something. Rationalization is a powerful motivator within our beings.

To rationalize is to keep the subject open, always making excuses for the circumstances that take place. Rationalization *never* brings closure. To reason is to bring closure. In Isaiah chapter 1:18 the Lord says:

Come now, let us reason together.

Never in the Bible does the Lord say, "Well, let's sit down and rationalize what we have done or what we are thinking about doing." God is a God of wholeness. We were created by Him, and in that creation He intended for us to be whole, not torn or separated into pieces. If one ingredient is missing from a recipe, it will not be right. It may be edible, but the taste of the end product is altered.

It is essential for us to learn to reason and to bring closure to situations. We cannot reason certain situations in our lives without the help of God. We cannot humanly do this, but God can. His Word says,

> *My thoughts are not your thoughts, neither are your ways my ways... As the heavens are higher than the earth, so are my ways higher than your ways and my thoughts than your thoughts.*
> Isaiah 55:8-9

God did not say this once but twice in these two verses. Something repeated is worth taking note of.

Without closure, we cannot move on from this personal holocaust. Are you ready to reason and bring closure to this area of your life? Do you want to know the fullness that the Lord has promised you in this life? If you did not then you would not still be reading, so come let us begin to reason together.

Polls have shown that more than 80 percent of women *would have* completed their pregnancies under better circumstances or with more support from the people they love.[2]

Looking back, I would have had the support and encouragement from my loved ones, but they could not support, encourage, or love me during this time because they did not know I was going through it. Our own silence can rob us of the very thing we may need at any particular time. We were not created to live in this world or survive on our own.

We have become a society of multiple faces. What face are you wearing today? Is it that "silent face" that needs to be broken? Silence can and will continue to torture you.

It is time to break the silence. People need to be educated. They need to know the truth. So many women have been deceived because information was withheld from them regarding their abortion. At the expense of a human life deception is many times the reason.

Hosea 4:6 says,
*My people are destroyed
from lack of knowledge.*

Satan would love for our lives to be led by deception. The enemy's attack against us is skillful. By observing us, he knows and looks for those moments of vulnerability he can exploit. Where there is deception, there is confusion, but where there is knowledge there is clarity and understanding. Think about it. How many things in your life would you have done differently if you had only known? But let's not get stuck in the "coulda, shoulda, woulda" pity party.

Are you drowning in the sorrows of the why's and why not's? Is the enemy's conduct going to dictate to you that your life have no joy, no peace, and no contentment? Are you a prisoner of hope?

American educator Booker T. Washington wrote, "There is no power on earth that can neutralize the influence of a high, simple and useful life." Every life is created for a purpose, so do not give up. There is hope! Press on and break out of the prison that has stolen your freedom.

Endnotes:

1. Guttmacher Institute, Parental Involvement, *State Policies in Brief*, April 2006, http://www.guttmacher.org/statecenter/spibs/spib_PIMA.pdf
2. Jones RK, Darroch JE and Henshaw SK, Patterns in the socioeconomic characteristics of women obtaining abortions in 2000-200

Chapter 4

Broken Silence

It was in the eighth year of my marriage that the silence of my abortion was broken. My husband and I were having an argument in the middle of the night, and out of my anger, I mentioned the abortion. Instantly there was nothing but silence. I was completely overtaken with fear. I lay there, holding my breath, anticipating what would come next. Finally, he spoke of how he often thought about the abortion and was sorry he forced me to have one. I could not respond to his comment. I had waited for years to hear him say he was sorry, and when he did, I could not speak.

At this time, we had a son who was four years old. I thank God for my son. He did not have to bless me with another baby, but God is a gracious God and His mercies are new every morning. The awareness of my son not knowing what it would be like to have a sibling was a reality. My husband had a vasectomy after my son was born, and I did not want to bring another child into an abusive home.

Two years later the abuse still had not stopped, and I divorced my husband after ten years of marriage and silence. Although I knew it was wrong to stay in an abusive relationship, I was now dealing with the guilt of a broken relationship, not as much a loss for myself, but a loss for my son, who would be affected by a broken home.

The divorce was ugly, as most are. The issues of shared parenting, child support, and emotional abuse continued.

The results of my abortion, although I could not see it at the time, involved issues of family relationships, self-identity, morality, and psychological and physical wellbeing. Negative emotions inevitably trickled into other areas of my life: more broken relationships, more heartache, and more negative behavior stemming from the regrets of my past.

Having indulged in regret, I am living proof that anxiety or worry produces the very condition we fear.

Emotional running continued and exhibited itself through my work. I would work as many hours as I could get and then "take call" to fill in the time I was not at work. My identity became my work. The busyness of my life allowed me to escape the emotions that would frequently surround me when I had time to think about them.

I was striving to provide a good home for my son, but the evidence of sadness in my son's eyes was like looking into the depths of the ocean. Dark and empty circumstances that had invaded my life were now affecting his. At times, it was so heart wrenching that I began to feel like I had failed him too. These feelings became so great that I left my second marriage, which had its own set of problems, to reconcile with my first husband. I felt I owed it to my son to give him what every child needs and wants in life: a family with a mom and a dad living together.

After a short time, it was evident that the abusive tendencies were still present and there was no change of heart in this man. I knew I did not want my son to grow up in an abusive home. My son and I were living on our own during this attempted reconciliation, so when I told my ex-husband that this was not going to work and we needed to get on with our separate lives, his response was anger and retaliation.

The next six years were a constant battleground. My ex-husband vowed to make my life as miserable as he could. I had lost one child and I was going to do whatever it took to keep from losing my son.

The manipulation I witnessed each time my son went to see his dad was crippling. The assault on my character was demonstrative and executed in front of our son on each visit. I clearly remember hiding in the corner of my kitchen, sliding down the wall as I wept uncontrollably, while listening to the verbal attack on me that our son heard time and time again.

This was not just a custody battle. This was an all-out war he had declared. When my son was old enough to go before the judge and decide where he wanted to live, my ex-husband again filed with the court for custody. I believe there is nothing worse than taking a mother's child from her. My ex-husband knew that the only thing that was significant to me was my son, and what better way to hurt me than by taking our son? At the age of thirteen, my son went to live with his dad.

I cannot explain to you the feelings I experienced. I felt as if someone had reached inside my very being and tore my heart out of my chest, ripping away every hope that I had.

Chapter 5

Pieces to Peace

I had been raised in a Christian home and knew in my mind that God was always there. I began to seek the Lord's will for my life with all my heart. I was in so much pain and just wanted to be whole. I felt torn in so many ways that my physical and psychological being needed a real touch from God. As I sought the Lord, He began to reveal some very important things to me.

The pieces and parts are what make one whole. What is whole? Webster's dictionary describes it as total, sound, intact, complete, unimpaired, entire, uncut, undivided, unbroken, and undamaged. The opposite of whole is partial, defective, imperfect, incomplete, fractional, part, limited, deficient, and unfinished.

The body, soul, and spirit are another definition of the word *whole*. Each part has a separate function. The body is our physical being. The soul comprises our emotional life. The spirit is the eternal part of us that will continue beyond the termination of our body's life. It is the most powerful part of our being: what we are all about, what we were intended to be and do in this life.

We all have an intended purpose and identity for our lives, even you. We can go through life searching for our dreams and what we believe is our purpose and still end up not knowing. Why is that? We make choices along the way that take us on a detour, but that does not mean we cannot get back on the right track. God has a dream and purpose for each of us and He never aborts a plan where He has planted a seed.

I was so emotionally torn and had felt so incomplete that I thought I would never feel any different. I had to choose to allow the Lord to do in my life what I could not do myself. I realized my limitations and knew I could not overcome them so I made a conscious choice to "let go and let God." And so, the journey continued.

The journey that I allowed the Lord to take me on has been ongoing. He showed me that the detour I had chosen to take could be aborted along with all the souvenirs I held onto for so long. The souvenirs of my own will, my own way of thinking, my independence, pride, anger, bitterness, and shame. I had to learn that the body, soul, and spirit must function in order and harmony if I am to be fulfilled as God intended.

My emotions influence the way I think and the choices I make. Likewise, the choices I make influence the way I think and act. Our thoughts and emotions are powerful forces.

One of the most important lessons I have learned is that I cannot make a decision based only on how I feel. Feelings are so unstable. We can be up and happy one minute and down in the dumps the next, it is like riding a giant roller coaster. Reflect for a moment on a decision you have made based on your feelings and the consequences you have had to live with because of that choice. The good news is that you do not have to continue to live out those consequences. There is hope and a future for you.

Jeremiah 29:11 says,
"For I know the plans I have for you," declares the Lord, "plans to prosper you and not to harm you, plans to give you a hope and a future."

Chapter 6

Freedom

A time came when I had the opportunity to travel to Miami with a group of women to work in a church with people primarily of Haitian decent. It was during that time that the Lord opened doors to allow me to share with others the work He had and was doing in my life and to relay to them the hope I had in Jesus. I had prayed and prayed as to what I should share that day, but I felt I had not really heard from God. Therefore, I stood up and began to share my experience. The pain, sorrow, and shame that had bound me for so long began to lift as the hope I had found in the Lord was now being seen by these women who so desperately needed the love and hope of Jesus.

Freedom for me came at a time of sharing with others. Recovery depends on one's willingness to tell her story and see God transform the pain. This involves being honest about what really happened and recognizing one's feelings and their meaning in your life. It is not about rationalizing what you want the meaning to be, but what the meaning truly is in your life.

I can sense others' pain and relate to the roller coaster effect of their feelings and thoughts. No, I cannot read their minds, but the saying "you cannot know what I'm feeling until you have gone through it yourself" is true. My circumstances are like no one else's, because I am like no one else. God made each of us unique. We are God's creation but have been shaped by the influences in our lives and the choices we have made.

The truth is there is no life spoken of in an abortion, only death. An innocent life is tried, judged, and executed without the thought of a fair trial. Sound familiar? Look at John 19. Jesus is tried of crimes and found innocent, but the people wanted judgment brought upon Him. Pilate said he washed his hands of the situation, and the people crucified Jesus.

Jesus knows; He has been there. He was taken at the hand of man but He lives at the right hand of the Father. These innocent infants were taken at the hand of man but are now loved, happy, and under the guardianship of our Lord and Savior. Jesus can fill that void in our lives that no one or anything else can.

Jesus went to the cross and bore *all* of our sins. He was so full of sin when He hung on the cross that His own Father could not look at Him. When the sky turned dark at 3:00 in the afternoon, Jesus felt forsaken by his own Father. He cried, "My God, My

From Pieces to Peace

God, why hast thou forsaken me?" You see, sin separates us from God. In order for us to have forgiveness, Jesus had to carry the burdens of our sins on the cross.

There is *no* sin too great that the Lord will not forgive us. He had to feel every pain and disappointment. He had to experience the loneliness and separation from God in order for us to be forgiven. He did that for me! He did that for you!

You may be asking, who is this God? Well, let me tell you. He is:

- my Rock
- my Refuge
- my Strength
- my Fortress
- my Deliverer
- my Shield
- my Lover
- my Light
- my Salvation
- my Provider
- my Friend
- my Redeemer
- my Peace
- my Husband
- my Joy
- my God
- my King

…to name just a few.

Jesus is everything to me because I am everything to Him. Jesus has set me free from the chains that pulled me down, held me down and tried to choke the life out of me. The Bible tells us that

> *He who the son [Jesus] sets free, is free indeed!*

I HAVE BEEN SET FREE! You can be free indeed!

Chapter 7

It Is Finished

Imagine the emotions Jesus felt the night He was found innocent of all charges yet was led to His crucifixion. Imagine the unfaithfulness He felt as His disciples betrayed Him. Imagine the pain He felt as they beat Him to the point of being unrecognizable, pulling on His beard until He bled, nailing His hands and feet to the cross, forcing a crown of thorns onto His head as the blood ran down His beaten body. What about the violation He felt as He hung naked on the cross as they spit on Him and mocked Him? Through His compassion and love, Jesus said,

> *Father, forgive them for they do not know what they are doing.*
> Luke 23:34

Jesus knows the physical, emotional, and mental burdens of sin we carry and the suffering we go through. He bore it all. He bore it all until there was no more to bear.

It is comforting to realize that Jesus knows about every detail in my life and cares about every one of them. He knows every hair on our heads as written in Matthew 10:30:

> *Even the very hairs of your head are numbered.*

He sees every lonely night when I lie awake in bed, He knows every concern about meeting my monthly obligations, He collects every tear that I shed, He feels every frustration I feel when there is no other human around to vent my cares to. He cares about every detail.

Jesus knew what the plan and purpose of His life here on earth entailed, and He willingly accepted God's plan. He knew that without His own sacrifice we would perish. Then in His weak, bloodied, beaten body He said with His last human breath,

"IT IS FINISHED!"

The word *finished* means paid in full. Jesus Christ paid the full penalty of our sins. When will you say "It is finished"? I am finished carrying the guilt, rejection, betrayal, and shame. I am finished burying the anger, fear, shame, and regret. I am finished with the negative effects and behaviors it has produced in my life.

When Jesus said, "It is finished" He meant "I have carried it all to the cross, and with My life I have paid the price." Not just some of my sin, but ALL of it. There is no sin that surpasses the forgiveness of Jesus. Nothing! But you must ask.

I heard an illustration from Anne Graham Lotz about forgiveness. So many times, we can forgive others, but we are not able to forgive ourselves.

Unforgiveness leads to bitterness, and the consequences of bitterness can and will affect our relationship with God, who is our only hope for an eternal future.

If Jesus died for all sins and said we are forgiven, yet we do not forgive ourselves, then are we placing our standards of forgiveness above God's standards? Are we better than God? Do we deserve His forgiveness? No, I do not deserve it, but I am willing to receive it. I am ready and willing to accept God's gift of forgiveness and say, "It is finished!" Are you?

Conclusion

I am not convinced that if the thoughts of past mistakes were to disappear, I would be a better person. The ability to remember, to feel, to see, to sense, and to reflect has been as much of a healing process for me as it was an ongoing nightmare. I believe each season of my life is preparing me for the plan and purpose for which God has set before me.

I know now where I do not want to go in life and what mistakes I will try not to repeat. There is that 20/20 vision again.

Martha Washington wrote, "I have learned from experience that the greater part of our happiness or misery depends on our dispositions and not on our circumstances." I choose to take my mistakes and failures and to apply them to my life in a positive way. I choose to focus my thoughts on the things above that are good, kind, and pure. The love and forgiveness that we receive from God cannot be kept a secret either. It illuminates our words, attitudes, and looks. Where the light of Jesus shines, there is no room for darkness or despair.

God has placed within us gifts that are not meant for us alone. If we are motivated by God's Spirit, He will lead us on a never-ending journey of,

> *...immeasurably more than all we ask or imagine according to His power that is at work within us.*
> Ephesians 3:20-21

We have no idea what He has in store for us. Reflecting back on my life, I can honestly say, "I have lived life." I have just wasted too much of it feeling guilty and not being able to forgive myself for my mistakes. I have wasted too much of my time feeling cheated.

I used to look around and wonder why my life could not be like someone else's. My desire to have a husband that would adore me and take care of me, dreams we could share and pursue and have the joy of accomplishing together, children who would grow up in a two-parent home filled with love and joy, watching them grow and become their own person, taking joy in their accomplishments and watching them learn life.

Nevertheless, when I look back, I have accomplished some of those and many others. My life took a different path in many ways, but not in all bad ways.

When my dad became ill with terminal cancer, I thought my life just stopped. He had been the only man in my life who was always there for me. It did not matter what I had done or not done. He still loved me. He always accepted me for who I was, regardless of the mistakes I had made. He was a man of very few words, but words do not always need to be spoken to express love.

The thought of losing him was devastating. That thought became a reality and life has been different ever since. In the many quiet times that we were able to share while he was ill, things were spoken and expressed in such a loving way that the mistakes and turmoil of life just did not seem to matter as much. The thing I was missing in life was life itself. It is such a precious thing.

It is not the details in life we should be so preoccupied with, it must be the people. The details will not remember a thing we did once we are gone, but the people we have touched will remember. It took the tragedy of my dad's death to bring me to the point of realizing life's importance.

It forced me once again to take time, to listen, to speak, to reflect, and to express. It took time. I was so fortunate to have had that time with him. Through his death, I have become a person who looks at people in my life, not just the details. I gave myself permission to openly grieve his death and at the same time celebrate where I am and what I have learned from his loss.

Things do not make a difference, people do. People who allow God to work in and through them make a difference. The circumstances and decisions of our lives can set us on a track, but it is the people

From Pieces to Peace

we become involved with that influence our lives. With the world in such turmoil and the unknown in our lives, there is only one person who can influence us beyond our imagination if we just ask Him to.

God can make a difference. His love, mercy, gentleness, kindness, grace, omnipotence— always knowing and understanding us—will make the difference. You say, "God can't know what I'm going through; He's God." But God created us in His own image and sent His only Son to bear all of our sins and sorrows on the cross. He experienced every thought, harmful word, disappointment, and pain we have been through. He knows! He lived it. He felt it. He carried it. He bore it, and He forgives it.

I am living proof that God can and does make a difference in one's life. I have never experienced such joy and peace as the Lord has so graciously given to me. He takes care of me because He loves me. I am content where I am for this time in my life because Jesus made me a promise that He will never break.

Psalm 103 is one of many scriptures that explain the great love of God for us.

Praise the Lord, O my soul;
all my inmost being, praise His holy name.
Praise the Lord, O my soul,
and forget not all his benefits—
Who forgives all your sins
and heals all your diseases,
Who redeems your life from the pit
And crowns you with love and compassion,

*Who satisfies your desires with good things so
that your youth is renewed like the eagle's.
The Lord works righteousness and justice
for all the oppressed.
He made known His ways to Moses,
His deeds to the people of Israel:
The Lord is compassionate and gracious,
slow to anger, abounding in love.
He will not always accuse, nor will He
harbor His anger forever;
He does not treat us as our sins deserve or
repay us according to our iniquities.
For as high as the heavens are above the earth,
so great is His love for those who fear Him; as
far as the east is from the west, so far has He
removed our transgressions from us. As a father
has compassion on his children, so the Lord has
compassion on those who fear Him; for He knows
how we are formed, He remembers that we are
dust. As for man, his days are like grass, he flourishes like a flower of the field; the wind blows
over it and it is gone, and its place remembers it
no more. But from everlasting to everlasting the
Lord's love is with those who fear Him, and His
righteousness with their children's children —
with those that keep His covenant and remember
to obey His precepts.*

We receive all of these blessings without deserving any of them. What a gift! If you are ready to accept the free gift of forgiveness, then take a moment and pray this prayer:

Dear Jesus, thank You for paying the price for all my sins. I repent of the sins in my life, even the ones I think are unforgivable. I believe that You died on the cross to forgive me of my sins so that I could someday be with You forever in heaven. I know my baby is in heaven with You and I will be joined with this child when I join You there. I renounce the enemy's words of deception in my life, and I choose to live by Your truth and Your Word. I am no longer bound by the anger, shame, bitterness, pain, or sorrow of my past sins because they are forgiven. I receive Your forgiveness and completeness in my life. Thank You for making the broken pieces of my past a place of peace for my future in You. I choose to accept Your forgiveness, love, and grace for my life. I will walk in Your plan and purpose for my life because I have a hope and a future in You. Thank You, Jesus. In the mighty name of Jesus I declare this, amen.

It is important to find someone who will pray and encourage you in your walk with the Lord. Find a church that teaches the Word of God and surround yourself with other believers.

Choose to focus your thoughts on the wonderful promises of God.

Knowing that God is never done with us, and that His plan and purposes will continue until He returns, be encouraged and continue to walk in the truth of God's Word, the Bible. Challenging circumstances will happen in our lives, but the Bible can and will help direct you in each one.

Do not become consumed with how big the challenge is. Become consumed with how big YOUR God is!

Celebration

As for our babies—no, we cannot bring them back, but we can rest in the peace of knowing that they are being held in heaven.

*And He took the children in His arms, put
his hands on them and blessed them.*
Mark 10:16

Look for Me

I do not understand
why I could not stay
Even when you felt
there was no other way

When I left you, Mom
I met my Big Dad
I was tattered and torn
And so very sad

He told me He created me
And I was His own
He would care for me now
Because I was home

In pieces I came
But He held me close
Away went the pain
and I became whole

I love you, Mom
And someday we will meet
When you come to heaven
Look for me
I will be playing at Dad's feet

From Pieces to Peace

*"I will turn their mourning into gladness;
I will give them comfort and joy instead of
sorrow," declares the Lord*
Jeremiah 31:13

Additional Resources

"Revisiting the Koop Report," *The Post Abortion Review,* Summer 1995, 1-3.

"Surgeon General C. Everett Koop's Statement on Post-Abortion Syndrome," *Life Cycle*, September 1989, 2.

Printed in the United States
95039LV00002B/469-999/A